# Collins

# Primary Social Studies for Antigua and Barbuda

**WORKBOOK**
**Kindergarten**

T0340562

Anthea S Thomas

William Collins' dream of knowledge for all began with the publication of his first book in 1819. A self-educated mill worker, he not only enriched millions of lives, but also founded a flourishing publishing house.

Today, staying true to this spirit, Collins books are packed with inspiration, innovation and practical expertise. They place you at the centre of a world of possibility and give you exactly what you need to explore it.

Collins. Freedom to teach.

Published by Collins
An imprint of HarperCollins*Publishers*
The News Building, 1 London Bridge Street,
London SE1 9GF

HarperCollins*Publishers*
Macken House, 39/40 Mayor Street Upper,
Dublin 1, D01 C9W8, Ireland

Browse the complete Collins Caribbean catalogue at
**www.collins.co.uk/caribbeanschools**

© HarperCollins*Publishers* Limited 2022
Maps © HarperCollins*Publishers* Limited 2022

10 9 8 7 6 5 4 3

ISBN 978-0-00-840289-1

Author: Anthea S. Thomas
Reviewer: Rochelle Richards
Publisher: Elaine Higgleton
Senior editor: Lucy Cooper
Development editor: Fiona MacGregor
Cover designers: Kevin Robbins and Gordon MacGilp
Artwork and cover image: Zavian Archibald
Typesetter: Jouve, India
Printed in the UK by Ashford Colour Press Ltd.

Collins would like to thank the following teachers who read and reviewed the materials in proof and gave valuable feedback:

Philip Lloyd, Curriculum Officer for Social Studies
Neilson Duberry
Francille Francis
Jacqueline Jackson
Vill Peters
Janice Walbroo

**Acknowledgements**
The Publishers wish to thank the following for permission to reproduce photographs. Every effort has been made to trace copyright holders and to obtain their permission for the use of copyright materials. The Publishers will gladly receive any information enabling them to rectify any error or omission at the first opportunity.

**Image acknowledgements**
Photogenesis Imaging Antigua & Barbuda: pages 35 mr, br, tr; 63 tm; 72; 86; 87; 90 tr; 91; 101 t; 106; 107; 108 tr, bl.
Alamy: pages 18 tl John Birdsall; 45 bl Roberto Moiola, robertharding; 83m StockbrokerXtra; 111 mt Image Broker (Florian Kopp).
All other images from Shutterstock
t=top, m=middle, b=bottom, r=right, l=left

# Contents

# Colour

Colour the boy. Colour the girl.

Date:

4

# Circle and say

## I am a boy.

## I am a girl.

boy

girl

Circle the sentence that relates to you and say
if you are a boy or a girl.

Date:

# Draw

Topic 1 About me   *Week 1*

Draw a picture of yourself. Write boy or girl.

Date:

# Match

Draw a line from the part of the body to the where they are on the boy and girl.

Date:

# Match

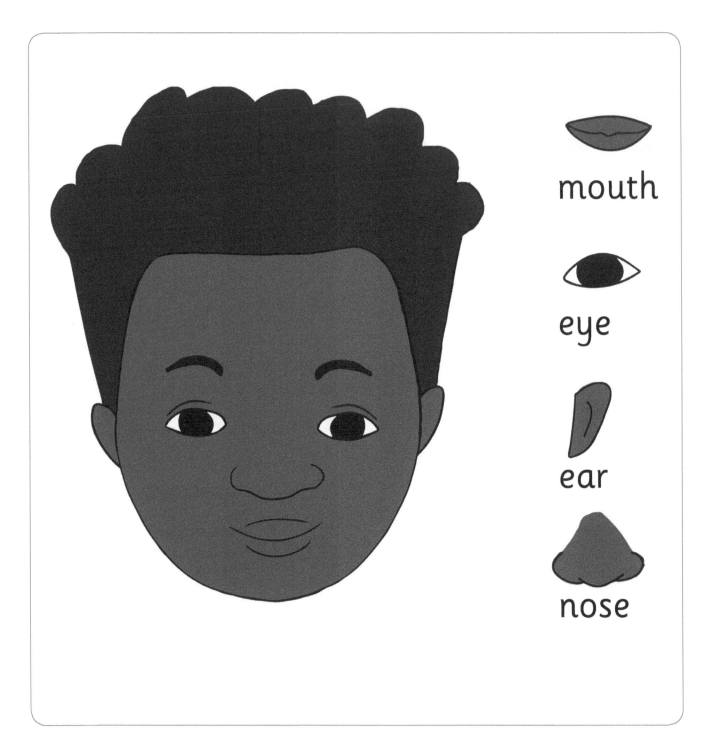

mouth

eye

ear

nose

Draw a line from the parts of the face to
where they are on the face.

Date:

# Draw

arms

legs

head

hands

feet

Draw a picture of yourself and then add lines from
the labels to where they are on your drawing.        Date:

# Look and say

What is the same? What is different?

Date:

# Trace and write

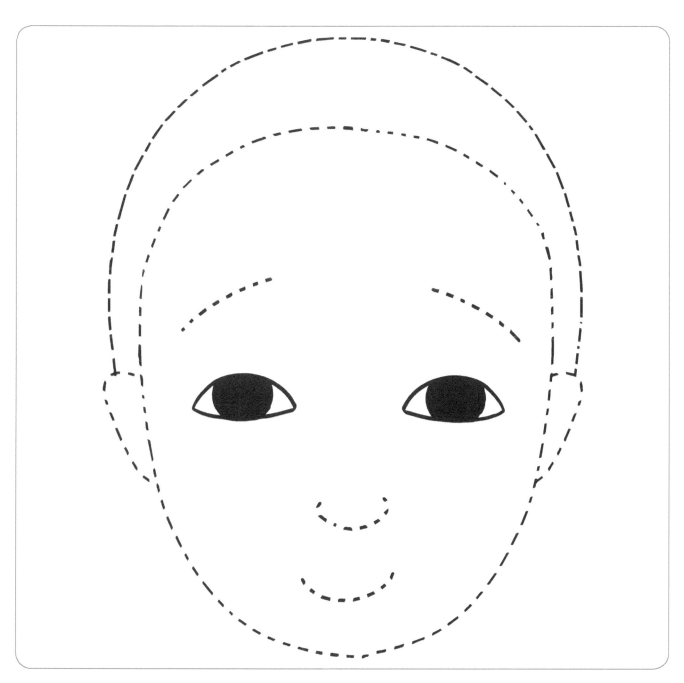

# I am special.

Trace the face and the writing.

Date:

# Colour

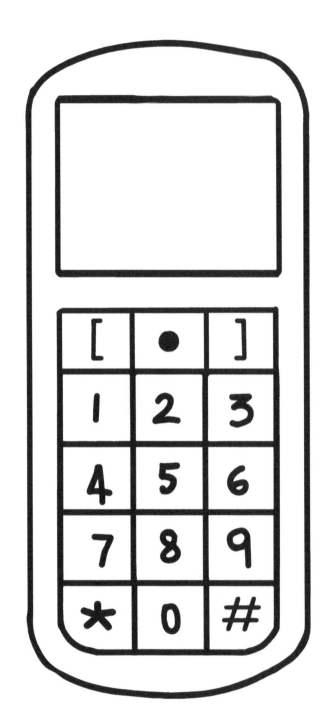

Colour in any numbers that are in your phone number.

Date:

# Circle

January     February     March

April       May          June

July        August       September

October     November     December

Circle the month of your birthday. Colour in the day.

Date:

# Colour and say

I am _____ years old.

Colour the candles to show how old you are.
Write the number.

Date:

# Design

Design your own birthday invitation.
You can use pictures or words.

Date:

# Tick and say

I can sing. ☐

I can dance. ☐

I can draw. ☐

I can help. ☐

What can you do? Tick the actions. Say the words.

Date:

# Draw

Draw a picture to show what you like to do.

Date:

# Match

Draw lines to match the pictures of a boy
and girl doing the same action.            Date:

# Tick

Tick the things you like to do. You can also colour the pictures.

Date:

# Colour and say

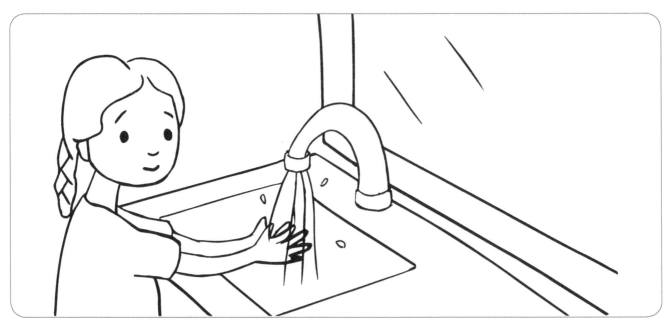

## She washes her hands.

## He brushes his teeth.

Colour the pictures. Say what the children are doing.

Date:

# Circle

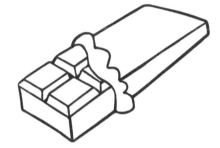

Topic 1 About me   *Week 5*

Circle the things you use to clean. You can also colour in the pictures.

Date:

# Circle and colour

Circle and colour the healthy food.

Date:

# Tick and say

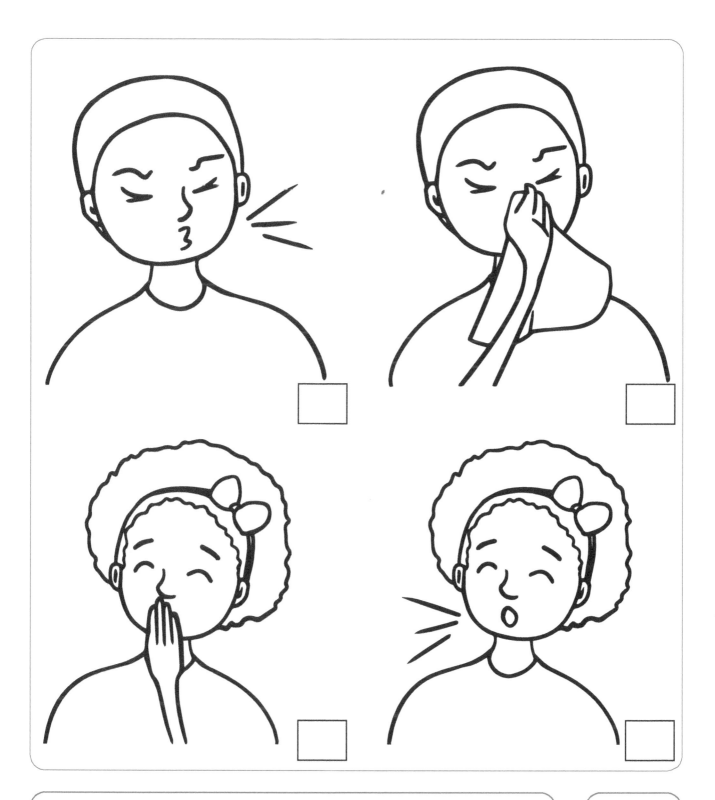

Tick and say what is the correct way to behave.

Date:

# Match

baby

mom

dad

brother

sister

Match the words to the people in the family.

Date:

# Paste or draw

Paste a picture of your family in the box, or draw
a picture of your family. Say the names of
each person. Write their names.          Date:

# Say and match

Tiana, my sister       Mom       Grandma

Me, Tiana's brother    Dad       Grandpa

This is the Thomas family. Say who everyone is and
match the words to the people in the picture.      Date:

# Count

## A big family

## A small family

How many people are there in each family? Count
and write the number. What size is your family?      Date:

# Colour

Topic 2 One happy family    *Week 2*

Colour in Auntie Dawn and baby K'Myah.
This is a single-parent family.                    Date:

# Draw

Draw a nuclear family: Mom, Dad and children.

Date:

# Colour and say

This is an extended family. Say who everyone is.
Colour the person who is wearing a hat.          Date:

# Colour

Colour in the father. Say what he is doing.

Date:

# Draw

Draw what work your mother does.

Date:

# Trace and say

mommy

daddy

mommy

daddy

m.

d.

Trace the words. Then write the words yourself
on the lines. Say the words.          Date:

# Colour and say

I sweep.

I wash.

I help.

I carry.

Colour the chores you do. Say the words.

Date:

# Match

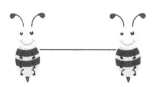

Match the person to their place of work.

Date:

# Draw

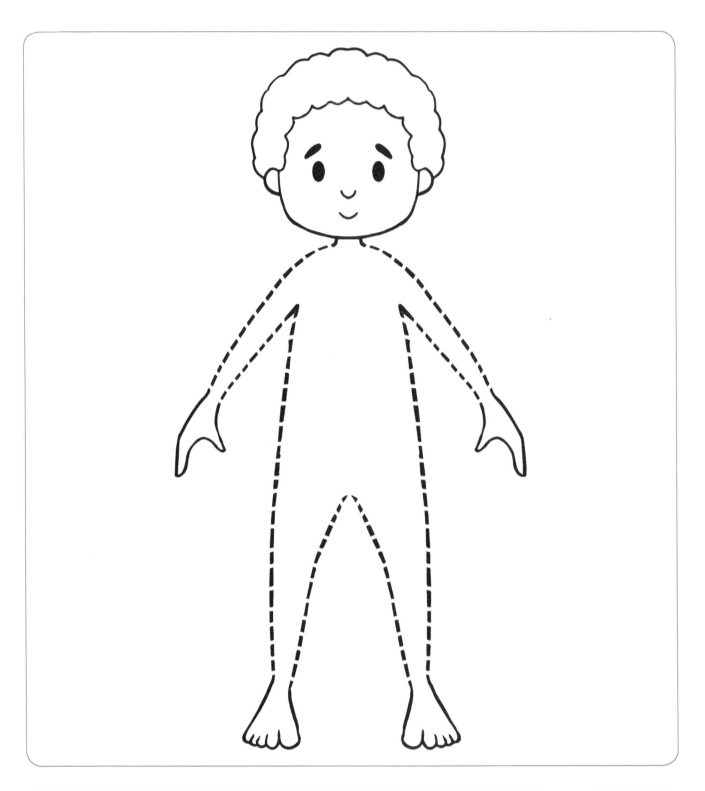

Draw nice clothes for this person to wear.

Date:

36

# Draw and say

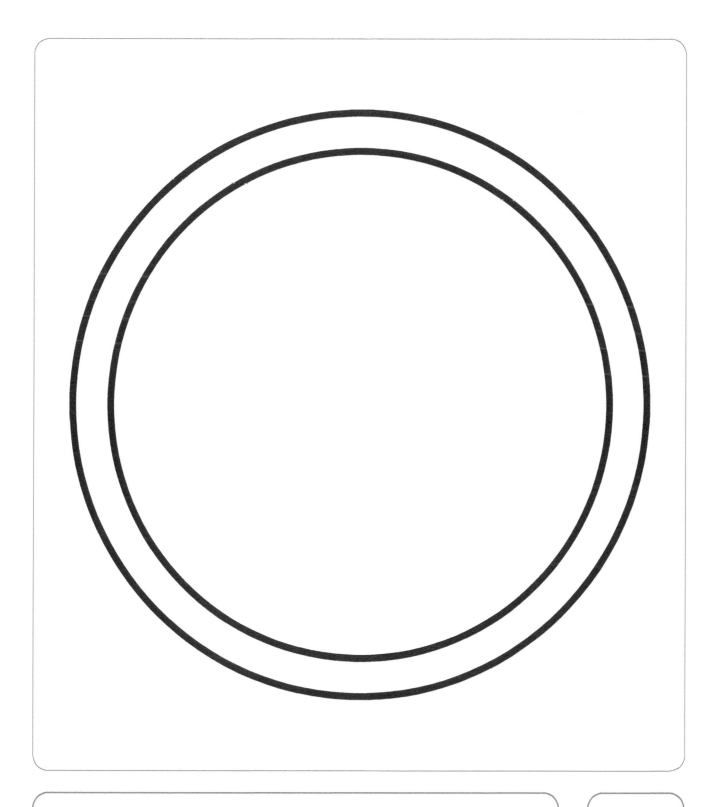

Draw a healthy meal on this plate. Say what the food is.

Date:

# Find and circle

Topic 3 My country    *Week 1*

Find the Caribbean on the world map.

Date:

Circle the Caribbean islands which include
Antigua and Barbuda.

Date:

# Find and circle

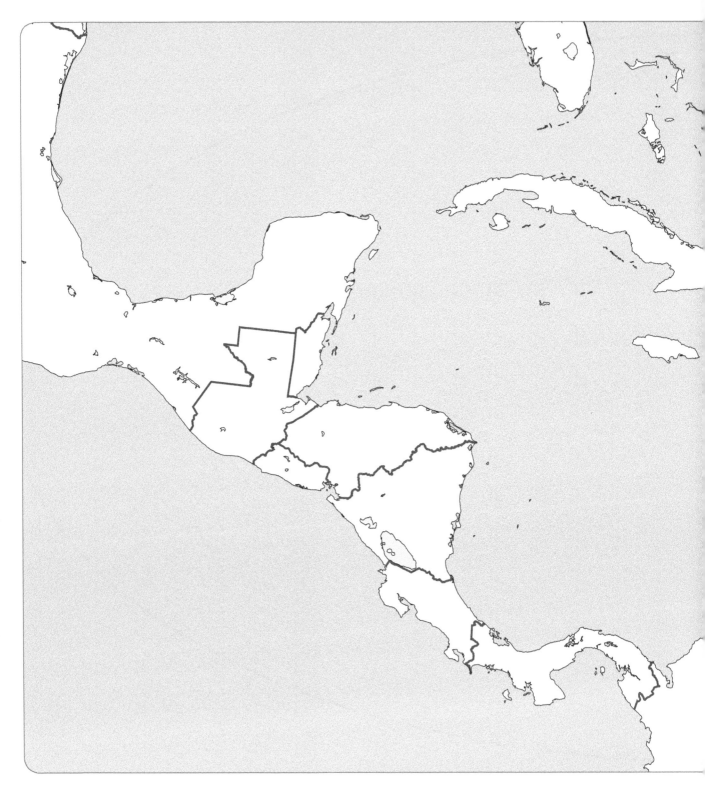

Find Antigua and Barbuda on this map of
the Caribbean.

Date:

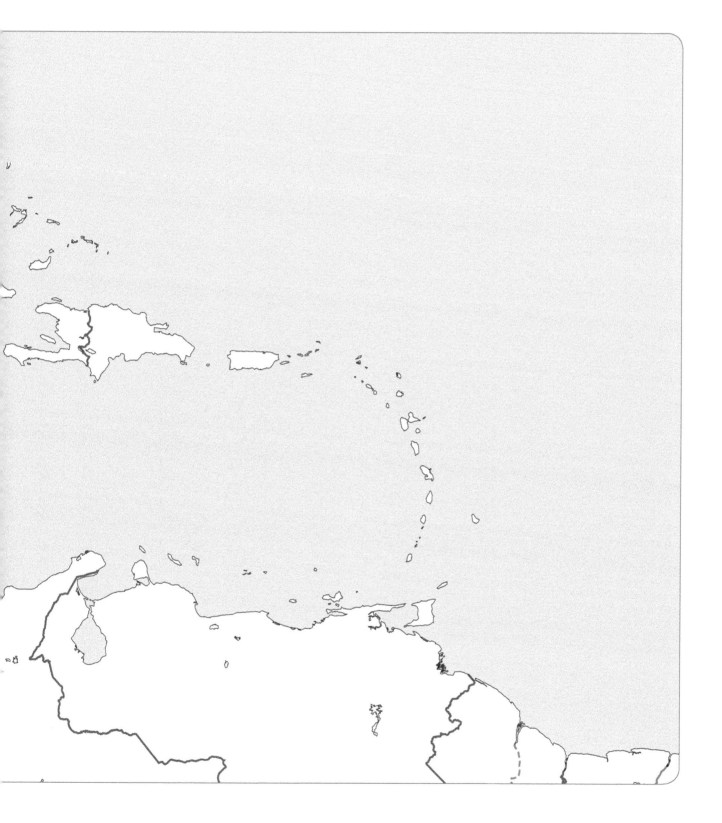

# Find and colour

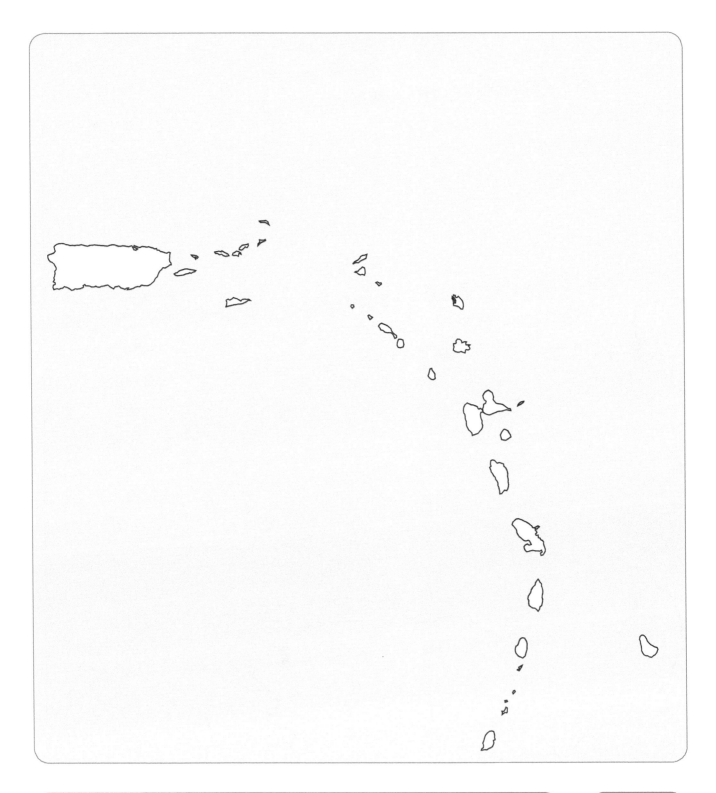

Find Antigua and Barbuda on the map. Colour them in.
Can you name any of the other islands?          Date:

# Trace

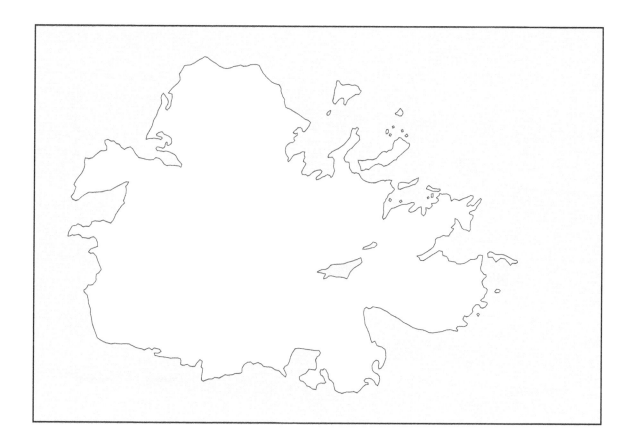

Trace the outline of Antigua and Barbuda. Colour them in.

Date:

# Find

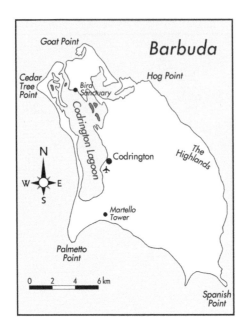

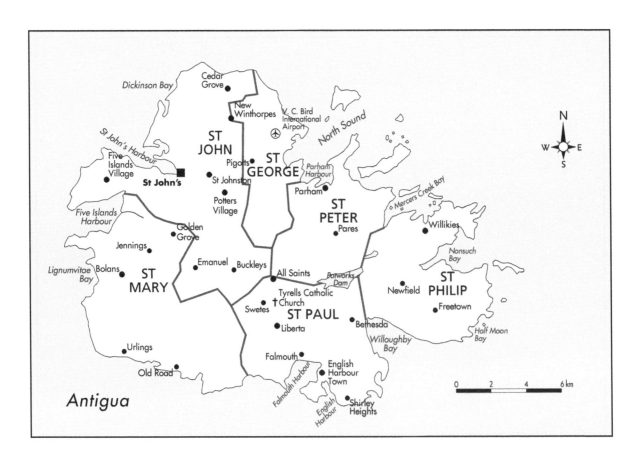

Find your parish. Colour in your parish. Mark where you live.

Date:

# Say

## St. John's Cathedral

## Potworks Dam

## Bird Sanctuary

## Nelsons Dockyard

Have you been to any of these places?
Say what they are. Your teacher will show
you where they are on the map.

Date:

# Look and say

## My address is:

_____

_____

Say where these envelopes and parcels are going. Write your address.

Date:

# Tick and say

0  1  2  3  4

5  6  7  8  9

Play phone bingo. Tick the numbers as you hear them.

Date:

# Match

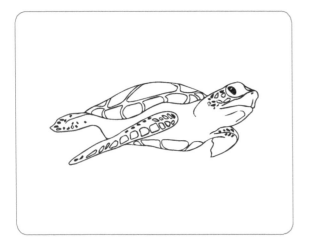

Match the outlines to the pictures of the animals.

Date:

# Colour and say

Colour the pictures. Say what they are.

Date:

# Circle

Circle the things that are national symbols.

Date:

# Colour and say

Colour the pictures. Say what they are.

Date:

51

# Colour

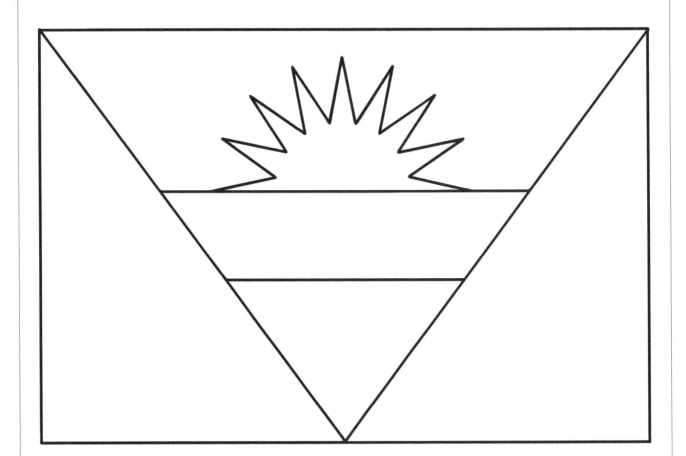

Colour our national flag.

Date:

# Choose

Which room is safer? Why? Tick the box next to the room that is safer.

Date:

# Put in order

Use the numbers to put the pictures in order.
Follow the pictures to say how to cross the road safely.     Date:

# Cross out

Cross out all the things that are not safe to play with.

Date:

# Follow

Follow the path to get safely to school.

Date:

# Colour and say

Colour and say what the rules are.

Date:

# Colour and say

Say what the good behaviour is.
Colour the pictures.

Date:

# Colour

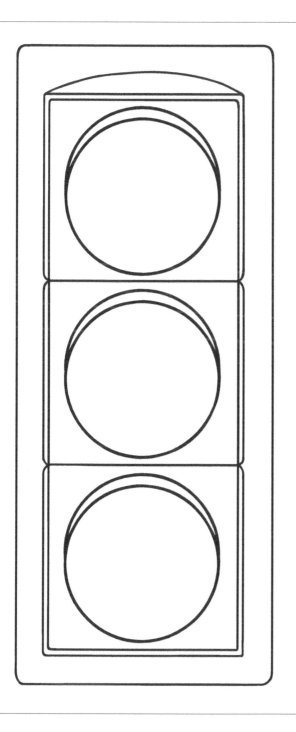

red

amber

green

Colour in the traffic lights.

Date:

# Match

Match the sign to the action.

Date:

# Draw

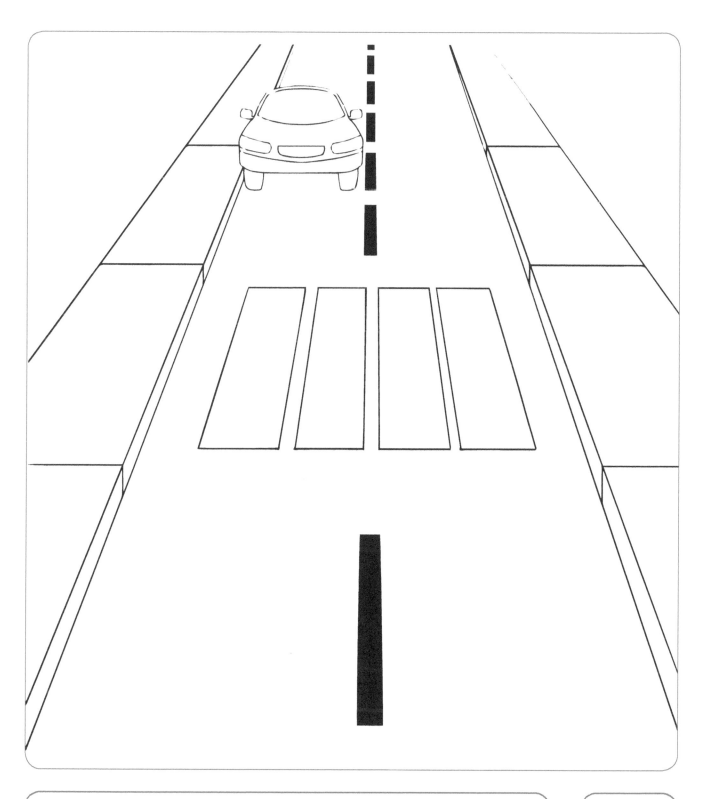

Topic 4 Watch out, be careful   *Week 3*

Draw children crossing the road in the right place.

Date:

# Colour and say

Colour in the road signs. Say what they mean.

Date:

# Match

police officer

doctor

fire fighter

Match the word to the person.

Date:

63

# Colour and say

Say what the nurse is doing. Colour in the pictures.

Date:

# Draw

Draw a picture of your school.

Date:

# Write

_____

_____

_____

_____

_____

Write the name of your school.

Date:

# Find and draw

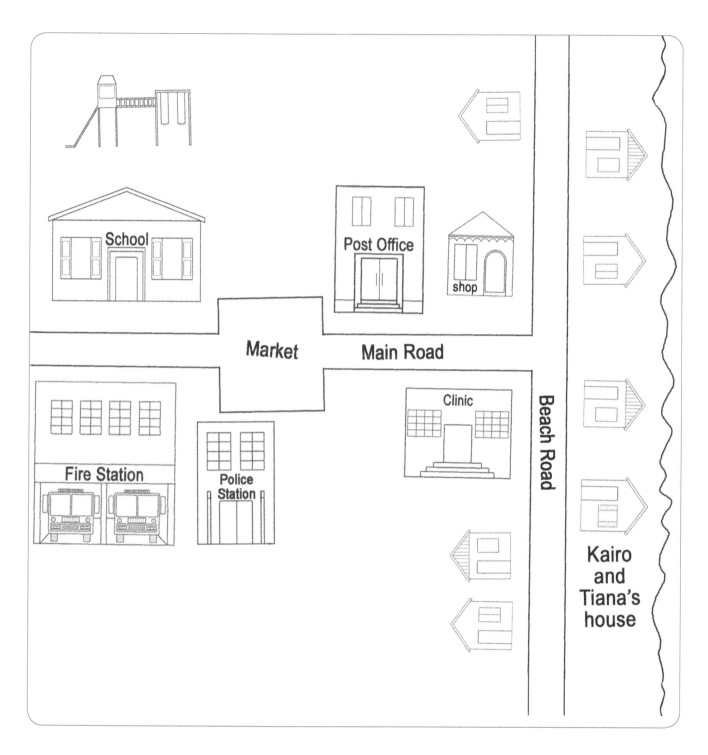

Find Tiana and Kairo's school. Draw a line from their house to the school.                    Date:

# Find and draw

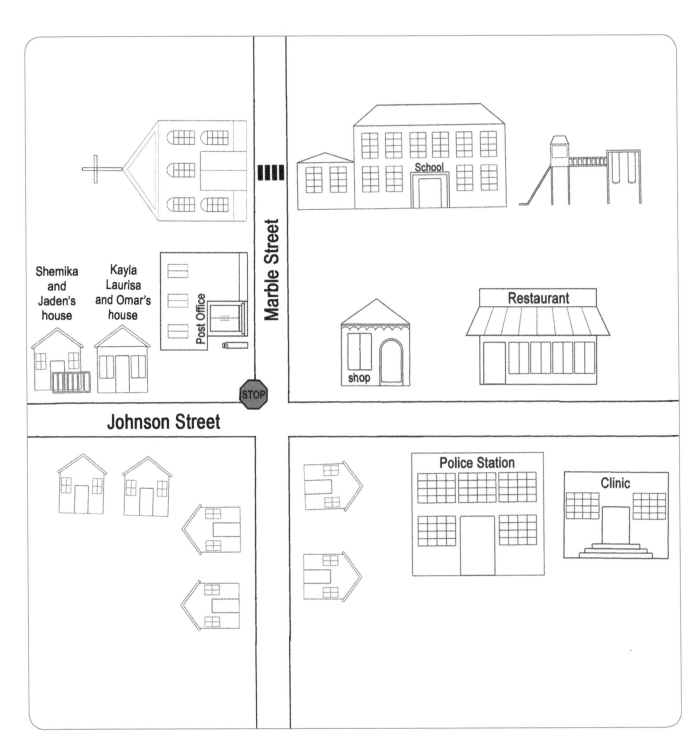

**Marble Street**

School

Shemika
and
Jaden's
house

Kayla
Laurisa
and Omar's
house

Post Office

STOP

**Johnson Street**

shop

Restaurant

Police Station

Clinic

Find the school. Draw a line from
Kayla's house to the school.

Date:

# Colour and write

teacher

t

Colour the teacher. Trace the word and then write
it yourself.

Date:

# Colour and write

principal     p

Colour the principal. Trace the word and then write
it yourself.          Date:

# Colour

Colour all the helpers in this picture.

Date:

# Match

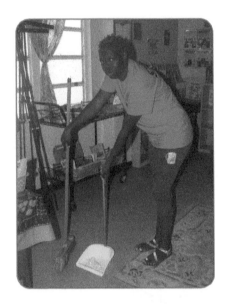

secretary

groundsman

janitor

Match the names to the helper.

Date:

# Spot the difference

Find five differences between these teachers. Colour them in.

Date:

# Match and say

soap       book       pencil

What goes in which room? Match the objects to where they are found in the classroom or the bathroom.        Date:

towel   toilet paper   chalk

What goes in which room? Match the objects to where they are
found in the bathroom or the classroom.          Date:

# Match and say

flowers    book    library card

What goes in which room? Match the objects to where they are
found in the library or the office.          Date:

pens     computer     magazines

Topic 5 At school   *Week 4*

What goes in which room? Match the objects to where they are found in the office or the library.          Date:

# Draw

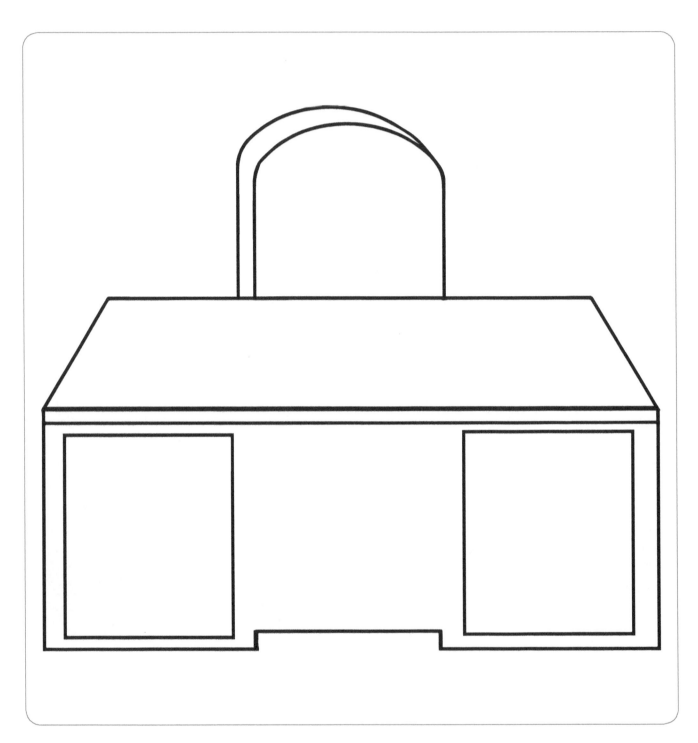

Draw the principal. Draw some objects on her desk.

Date:

78

# Colour and match

| listen | read |
|--------|------|

Who is reading? Who is listening? Match the people
to the word. Colour the picture.          Date:

# Draw

Draw yourself reading a book.

Date:

# Sing

Say or sing the rhyme on page 46 of the Student's Book.
Colour in the picture.                        Date:

# Write

My name is _____.

My name is _____.

I live in _____.

I live in _____.

My school is _____.

My school is _____.

Write your name and where you live. Write the name of your school.
Practise writing the full sentence.                    Date:

# Match

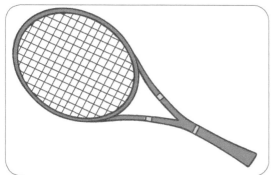

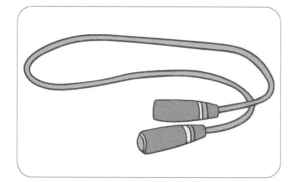

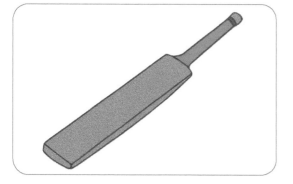

Match the item to the game.

Date:

# Say and match

## 1. Be respectful.

## 2. Be responsible.

## 3. Be kind.

## 4. Give others their privacy.

## 5. Play with children your own size.

Say the expectations and talk about what they mean.
Which two expectations are being shown on the next page?     Date:

Draw lines to match the pictures to two of the expectations on the other page.

Date:

# Tick

church ☐

shop ☐

school ☐

clinic ☐

Say what each building is and tick the ones that you have in your neighbourhood.      Date:

police station ☐

fire station ☐

post office ☐

playground ☐

# Compare

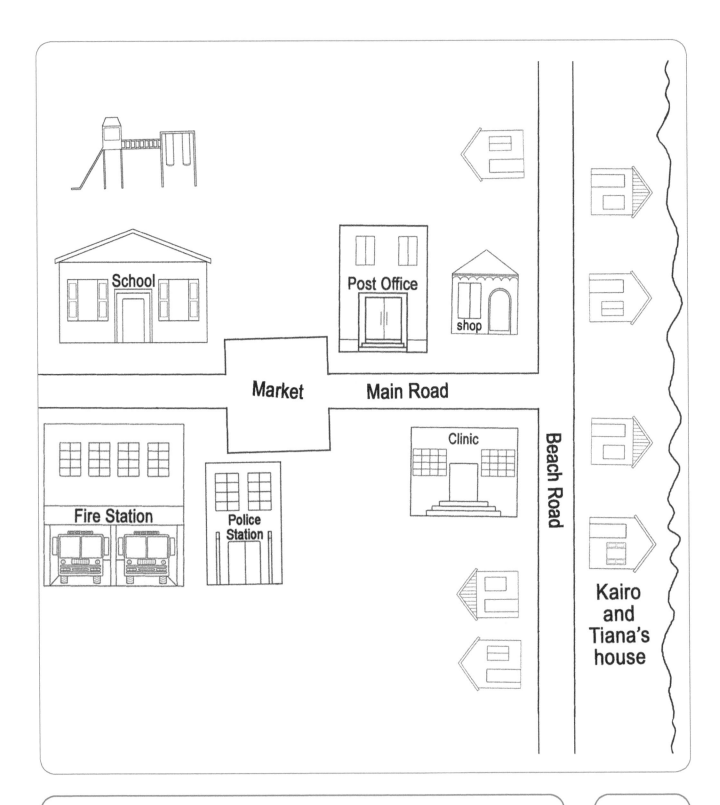

Look at the street plan on this page and the next.
What is the same?                    Date:

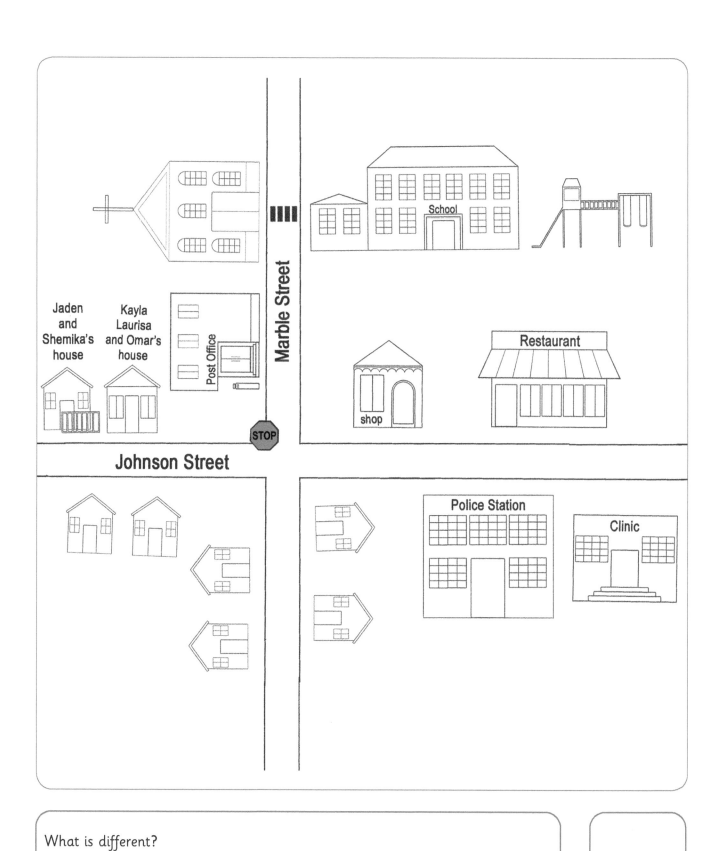

What is different?

Date:

# Match

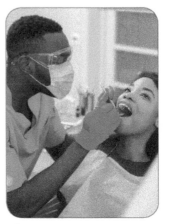

| nurse | doctor | dentist | fire fighter |

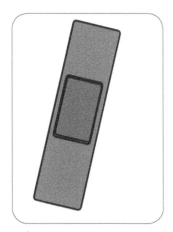

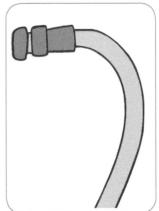

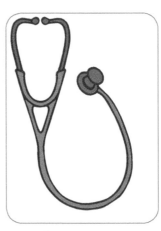

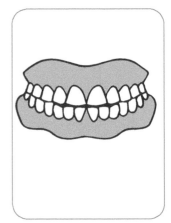

| plasters | hosepipe | stethoscope | false teeth |

Match the worker to the things they use to help people.

Date:

police officer

postwoman

shopkeeper

barber

police hat
and whistle

letters in
envelopes

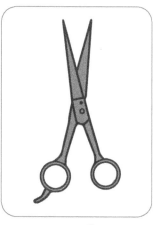

a pair of
scissors

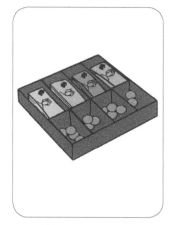

a shopping
till

Match the worker to the things they use in their job.

Date:

# Find and colour

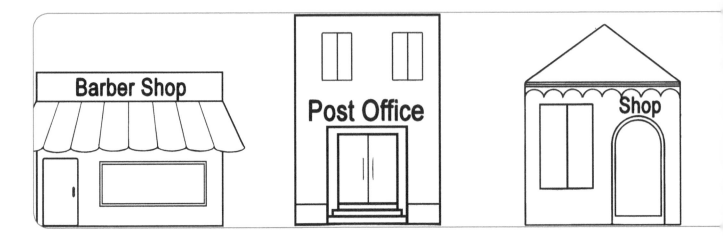

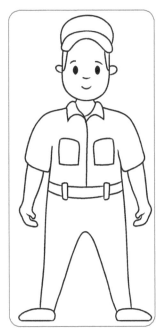

postman

shopkeeper

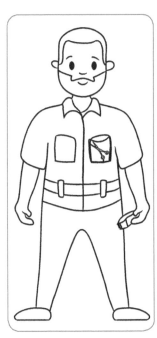

barber

Help the workers to find their workplace. Colour in the buildings and their worker the same colour.   Date:

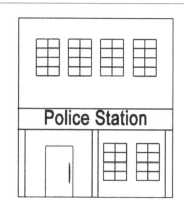 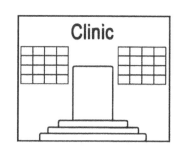 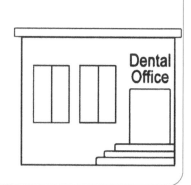

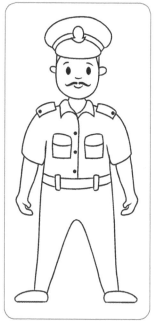

police officer

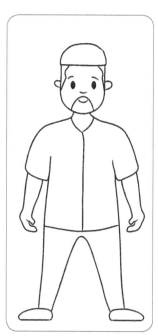

dentist

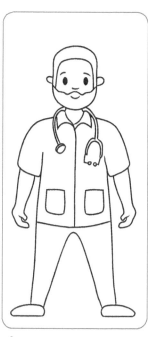

doctor

# Colour

Topic 6 My community   *Week 3*

Colour the places where people can live.

Date:

# Circle and say

walk / ride

walk / ride

Circle the correct word to say what the people are doing. Say the word.

Date:

# Find and colour

Find the vehicles that are the same.

Date:

Colour the same vehicles the same colour.

Date:

# Colour by numbers

1  red   ●

2  yellow   ○

3  blue   ●

4  green   ●

Colour the parts of the car, using the
number key provided.          Date:

# Draw

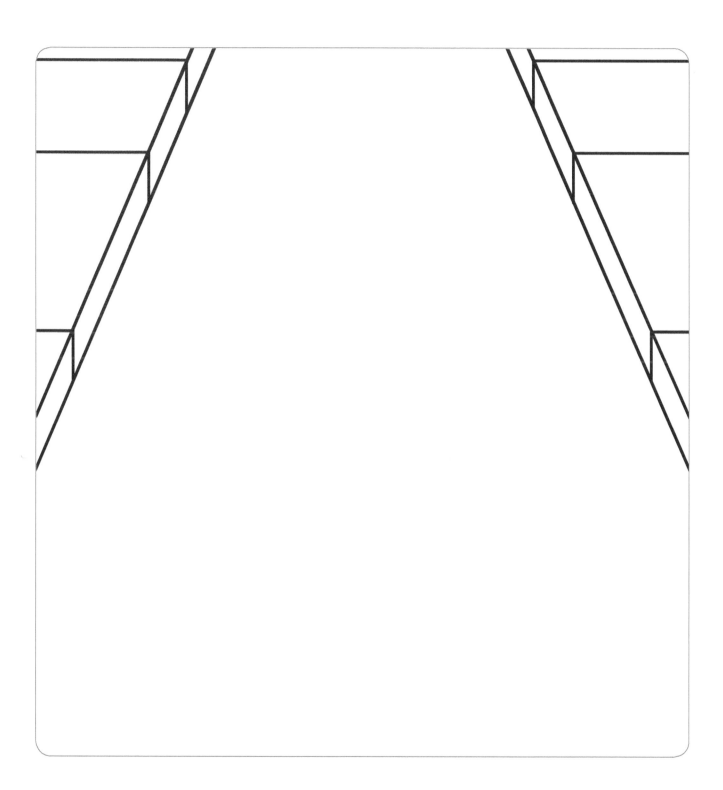

Topic 7 Transportation   *Week 2*

Draw a car on the road.

Date:

# How many?

How many people on the bus? Count and write
the number in the box.                    Date:

# Match

Topic 7 Transportation  *Week 2*

Match the transport to where you would find it.

Date:

# Count

How many boats can you count? Write the number
in the box.                                    Date:

# Draw

Fill the cart by drawing what you would take to market.

Date:

# Colour and say

Which animals can be used for transport? Colour and say.

Date:

# Follow

Follow the path to help Mom carry her heavy bags home.

Date:

# Match

Topic 7 Transportation   *Week 4*

Match the transport to where you would find it.

Date:

Talk about each of these places. Have you been to
any of them? What do we do at them?          Date:

# Match

Match the worker to the transport on the next page.

Date:

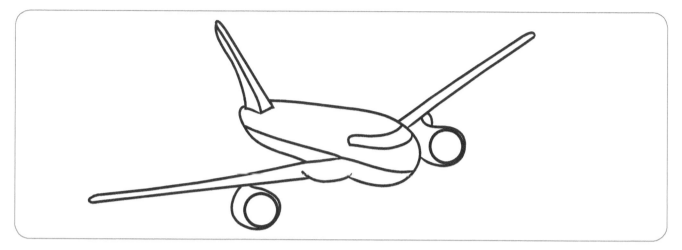

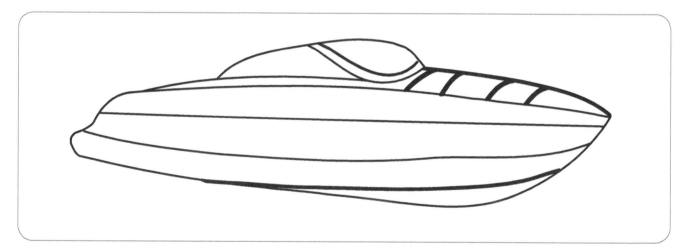

Colour the transport.

Date:

# Colour and say

Topic 8 Communication   *Week 1*

Colour the people. Say what they are doing.

Date:

# Match

draw

draw

sing

sing

talk

talk

write

write

Match the words to the pictures. Trace the words.

Date:

# Circle and say

Circle all the types of communication. Say what they are.

Date:

# Draw

Draw a birthday card. Use words or pictures.

Date:

# Colour

Topic 8 Communication  *Week 2*

Colour in the sign for love.

Date:

# Copy and draw

Copy these emojis. Draw some of your own.

Date:

# Write

Write a secret message. You can use words, pictures or signs.

Date:

# Match

Match the person to the object.

Date:

# Colour by numbers

1 red

2 yellow

3 blue

Colour in the radio. Use the number pattern.

Date:

# Draw

Draw your favourite TV programme or TV character.

Date:

# Count and tick

Count the phones. Tick the ones you like.

Date: